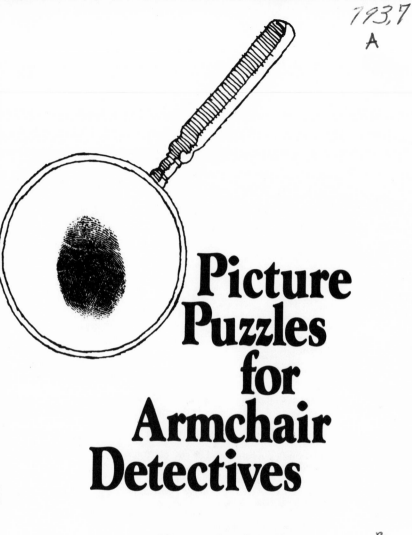

Picture
Puzzles
for
Armchair
Detectives

Doug Anderson

Sterling Publishing Co., Inc. New York
Distributed in the U.K. by Blandford Press

Other Books of Interest

Brain-Teasers and Mind-Benders
Calculator Puzzles, Tricks and Games
Eye Teasers
Metric Puzzles, Tricks and Games
Mind Teasers
Seeing Is Not Believing
Super-Colossal Book of Puzzles,
    Tricks and Games

Library of Congress Cataloging in Publication Data

793.7
A

Anderson, Doug, 1919–
    Picture puzzles for armchair detectives.

    Previously published as: Eye spy. c1980.
    1. Puzzles—Juvenile literature.   2. Visual
perception—Juvenile literature.   I. Title.
GV1507.D4A53   1983   793.73   82-19344
ISBN 0-8069-7718-3 (pbk.)

    ISBN 0-8069-4670-9 trade
          0-8069-4671-7 library

Published in 1983 by Sterling Publishing Co., Inc.
Two Park Avenue, New York, N.Y. 10016
Originally published in hardcover under the title
Eye Spy © 1980 by Sterling Publishing Co., Inc.
Distributed in Australia by Oak Tree Press Co., Ltd.
P.O. Box K514 Haymarket, Sydney 2000, N.S.W.
Distributed in the United Kingdom by Blandford Press
Link House, West Street, Poole, Dorset BH15 1LL, England
Distributed in Canada by Oak Tree Press Ltd.
% Canadian Manda Group, 215 Lakeshore Boulevard East
Toronto, Ontario M5A 3W9
Manufactured in the United States of America
All rights reserved

Contents

How to Use this Book

Detectives need sharp eyes and good memories. They must train themselves to note quickly all the details at the scene of a crime and to remember these clues so that they can use them to solve the crime.

In this book you are the detective. These games and puzzles will help you to develop your powers of observation, memory and deduction. What *do* you see? What *did* you see? What does it *mean*?

There is a time limit for each puzzle, and under the picture—or on the following page—are questions for you to answer. Keep a pencil and paper handy and a watch or clock for timing yourself. Or a friend could time you and check your final score. You can do the same for him or her—then compare scores to see who wins. Answers and scores are in the back of the book to show just how good a Sherlock Holmes or Miss Marple you are.

After you complete all the puzzles, go back and do them again. You will be surprised at the details you missed the first time round. A few of the puzzles are designed to have more than one solution and each time you do them you will be able to cut the time it takes to find the answers.

This book will not get you a badge on the police force; nor will you be able to open your own private detective office. It will, however, train you to "look sharp," and this is a skill you can use in everyday life. Whether you become an engineer, a bank clerk, a fashion designer—whatever—if you see more, you'll enjoy more, and maybe eventually know more than those around you.

1

Private Eyes

WANTED!

JAMES JONES ALIAS "MUGSY"
AGE: 37 WEIGHT: 156
HAS SCAR ON RIGHT CHEEK
HAIR: BLACK   HEIGHT: 6' 7"
EYES: ONE BLUE, ONE BROWN

As a detective, you see a lot of "Wanted" posters.
Study this one for two minutes, then turn the page.

6FT.

5FT.

4FT.

Which of the suspects in the line-up

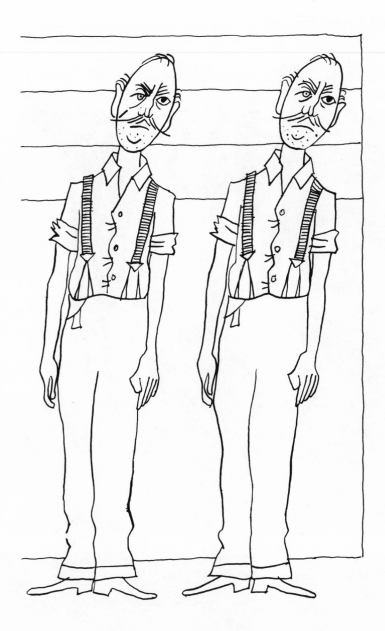

is the criminal on the poster?

THEY'RE OFF. . . .

. . . Or they will be if they ever reach the starting line. Study these crazy racers for three minutes. Then turn the page to see who won.

Only one racer reached the finish line. All the others dropped
out. Can you tell by these tracks who won?

A TIP

This letter was sent to the police. Study it for one minute and
see if you can figure out:

1. How was it written?
2. On what day was it written?
3. What is the stolen item?
4. Are there any misspelled words?

TO **THE** COPS

If you **look** INSIDE

the **OLD FORGE**

Tomorrow Saturday

You can **Find** the

Missing *Mona Lisa*

THE " **The**if "

15

THE CASE
OF THE
EMPTY EAR

You are the "private eye" hired by Mrs. Vanderposh to guard her jewels. Suddenly at the party, she misses one earring. Has someone snatched it? Or can you find it in her jewelry box? (*1 minute*)

HE SHOULD HAVE WORN GLOVES

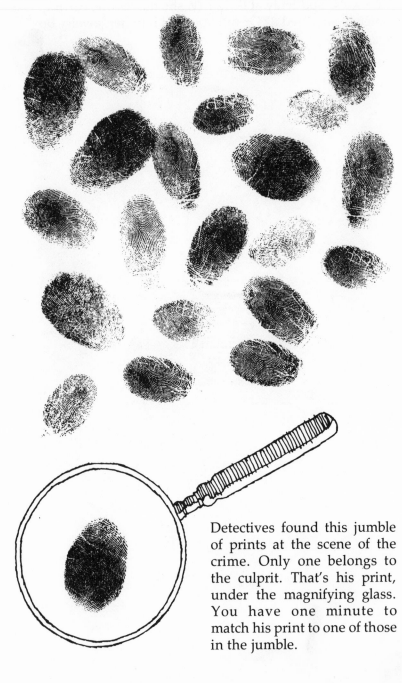

Detectives found this jumble of prints at the scene of the crime. Only one belongs to the culprit. That's his print, under the magnifying glass. You have one minute to match his print to one of those in the jumble.

2

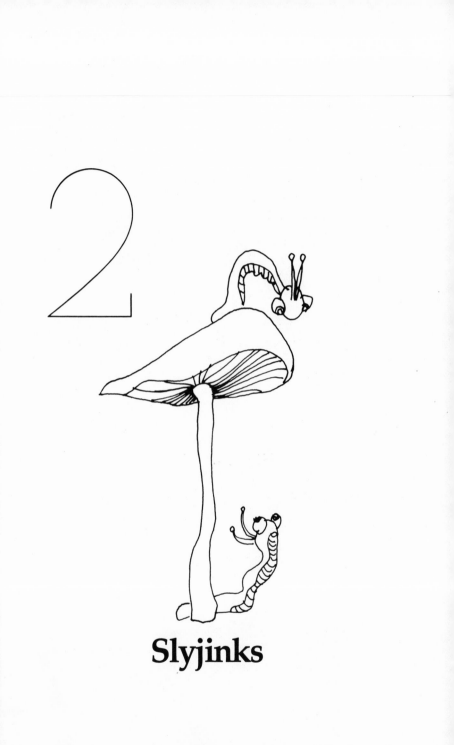

Slyjinks

ANYONE HOME?

Can this be Dracula's castle? Go up the path (if you dare) and peek in the window . . .

Yes, it's his pad, all right. Can you find the

Drac himself and his Gal Friday? (*3 minutes*)

THE GET-AWAY CAR

A good detective might be a little suspicious of this gas guzzler parked—illegally—near the scene of the crime.

Memorize as many details as you can in two minutes, then turn the page.

1. What state is the car from?
2. What is the license number?
3. What ornament is on the hood?
4. What is the monogram on the door?

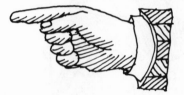

PUT A HANDLE ON IT

Herbert, the Handle-Grabber, boasted that he took home a souvenir from every job he ever pulled. Police identified the handles from all his other crimes, but these were left. Can you name the eleven items missing these handles? (2 *minutes*)

Study these pages for four minutes:

1. How many of the butterflies are exactly alike?
2. There is something in the picture which is not a bug or a butterfly. What is it?
3. Is anything wrong with one of the butterflies?

"Three Fingers" spent so much time in prison that he never did learn how to spell. When he had to write a letter to his partner in crime, he used pictures from the newspapers for most of the words. You have two minutes to figure out his message.

3

The Eyes Have It!

MASQUERADE

Seven guests are at the masquerade. Can you tell from their hats what characters they are impersonating? (*2 minutes*)

MAD HATTERS

MRS. TIMBUCK

Mrs. Timbuck bought a crazy hat. Mrs. Tew tried to copy it exactly. But has she?

MRS. TEW

Compare the hats for two minutes and see how many differences you can find.

THE DEFECTIVE DETECTIVE

All of the merchandise on these two pages was returned to the store for refunds. Can you detect the flaw in each one? (*2 minutes*)

TIME AND TIME AGAIN

You have four minutes to study these timepieces. Then, without looking at the picture, test your memory:

1. How many clocks are in the picture?
2. How many watches are in the picture?
3. How many are exactly on the hour?
4. How many have Roman numerals?
5. How many have "second" hands?
6. What is wrong with one clock?

FILM STRIP

After a hard day's work, Mr. Bome is headed for his home at 106 Jane Lane. Can you help him on his way by putting the five pictures in their correct order? (*4 minutes*)

1

2

3

4

5

THE LOST HEIRESS

There was a rich lady named Potter,
Who searched for her runaway daughter,
To make her her heir.
She looked everywhere—
Except in the one place she ought-er!

Can you find her daughter? (*1 minute*)

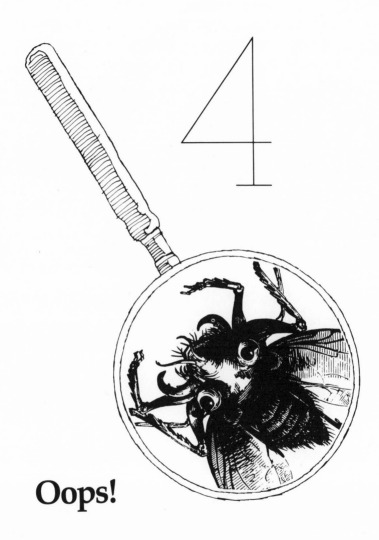

4

Oops!

THE TERRIBLE TWINS

When the supermarket was robbed, the police recognized the handiwork of the Terrible Twins. The twins tried to get lost in the crowd. Can you finger them in two minutes?

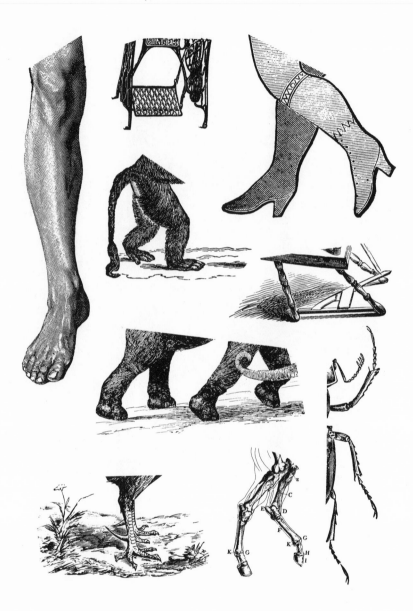

Can you tell who or what owns these legs? (*1 minute*)

MONSTER MIX AND MATCH

Minnie Monster and her friends on the next two pages are made up of odd bits and pieces which Dan, the Demented Doctor, found lying around his laboratory. Spend two minutes on each page and see if you can list the ingredients Dan used in each monster.

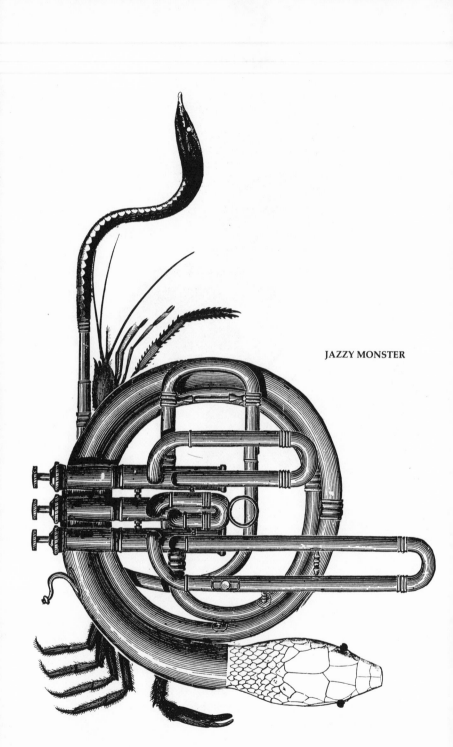

JAZZY MONSTER

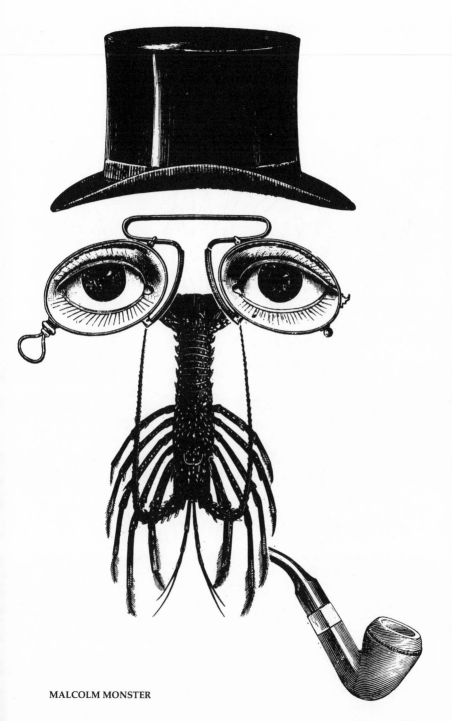

MALCOLM MONSTER

ON THE LOOSE

Three animals escaped from the zoo and managed to hide in the bushes of this tropical park. They are apt to annoy the tourists.

Can you find them in one minute?

THE GHASTLY GARDEN

They say that Old Mr. Tumbleweed keeps ghastly things in his garden, though no one is willing to say what.

Do you see anything horrible? (2 *minutes*)

ODD BIRD

Birds of a feather stick together, but this bird is stuck together from parts of four birds. Can you name them? (*1 minute*)

Sneaks

CHANGE OF HEART

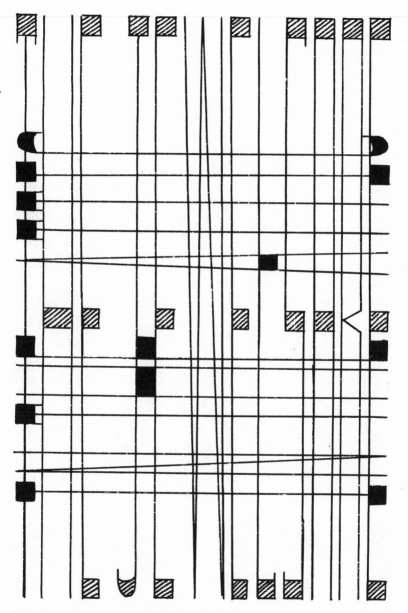

Celestine, the sneak thief, decided to go straight. She left this message for the police, but out of habit, she wrote it in code. Can you decode it in two minutes?

THE UNLOCKED WINDOW CAPER

This quiet living room contains several valuable antiques. This is how it looked before the burglar came.

The same living room ten minutes later. See if you can discover what was stolen. After two minutes, turn the page.

One of these odd-looking people is the burglar.

As the detective assigned to the case, which one would you arrest?

MONSTER RALLY

The Head Ghoul has called for a get-together. All the uglies are to meet at midnight down in the swamp and bring their

own lunch. Study this pesty parade for a minute, then turn the
page. . . .

How many monsters are on their way to the picnic? (If your answer is *six*, look again.)

SECRET PLANS

On breaking into Professor Moriarty's study, you and Doctor Watson find that he has once again escaped the law and disappeared with the Crown Jewels. But wait! He burned something before he left, and he missed some pieces of paper. They may tell where the jewels are hidden. They seem to be plans . . . what are they for: A railroad track? A bridge? A fence? A cathedral? (*1 minute*)

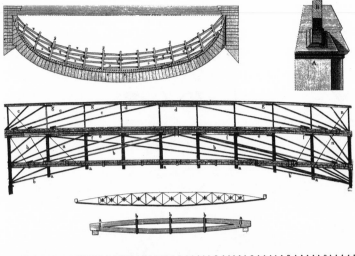

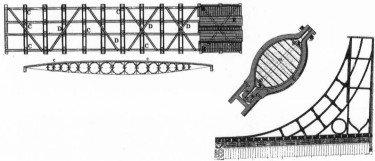

DOUBLE EXPOSURE

The members of the Jack-the-Ripper Fan Club have gone un-
derground, and no one knows how many of them are still
around. This photo is said to show the entire JR Club. How
many are there? (*2 minutes*)

Genius at Play

THE WOULD-BE PICASSO

The artist has called his painting "Making Sense." See if you can figure out what he means. (*3 minutes*)

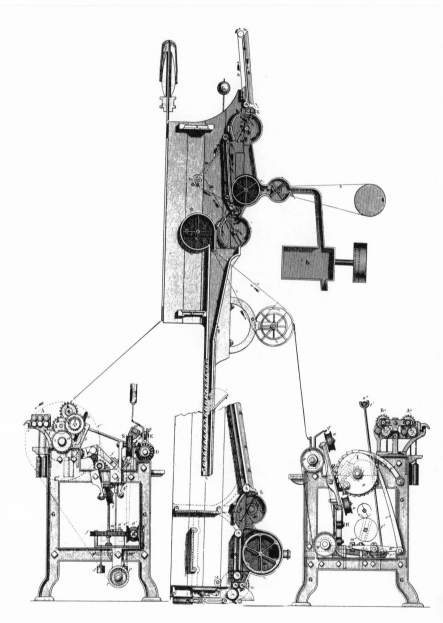

Mr. Fix-It invented this very complicated gadget. It doesn't work, but it looks good.

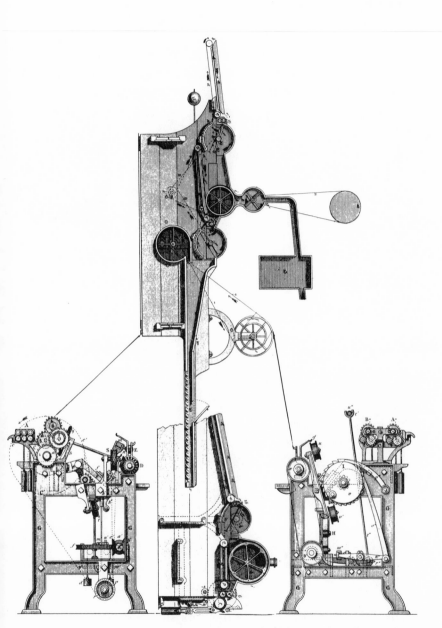

Mr. Copicat tried to make one exactly like it, but his spies forgot to tell him about four parts. Can you tell which parts are missing? (*2 minutes*)

NAME THE MONSTER

Colonel Mustard has made this monster, but can't think of a name for him. If you identify five items he used in making the monster, the first letters of each one just may spell out a name. (*2 minutes*)

MASTER MIND

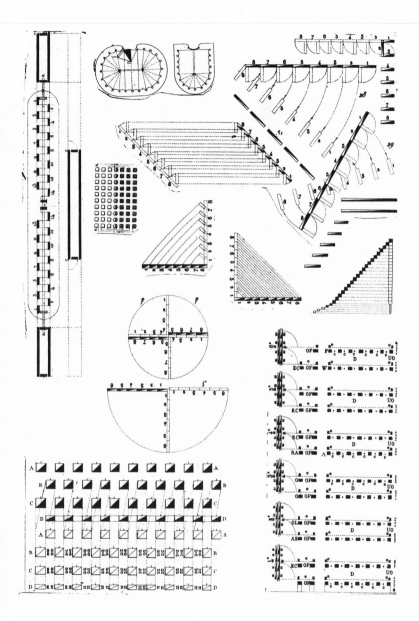

These plans were found in a very old trunk. Study them for a minute; then turn the page.

You have one minute to pick the creator of these plans. Was he: A city planner? An architect? A sports promoter? A general?

?-STAR GENERAL

This military genius has lost his stars. In two minutes, how many can you find?

THE CAN-CAN MYSTERY

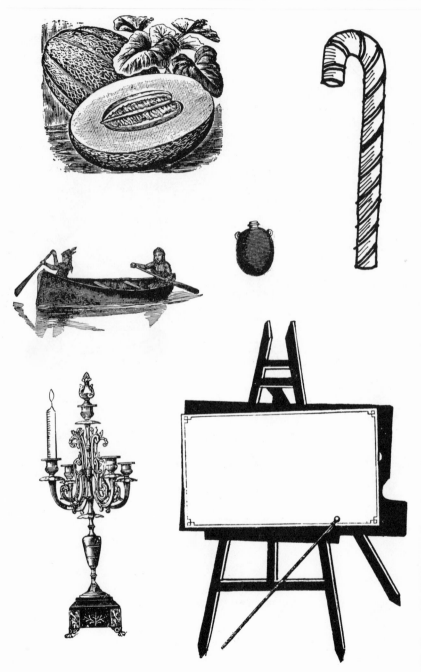

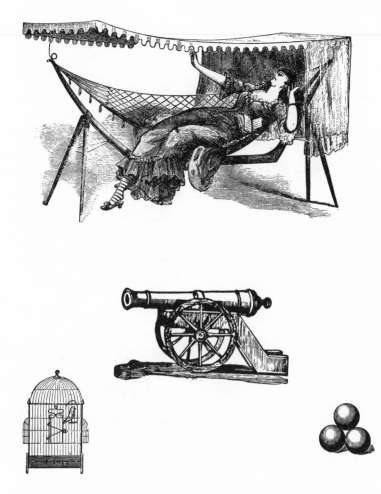

The ten items on these pages have "can" in their names. How many *can* you identify in three minutes?

MIXED-UP MENAGERIE

There are not three animals here, but seven. Can you unscramble them? (*2 minutes*)

Close Encounters

FIND THAT MAN!

You are tailing a suspect. His description:
 MALE, ABOUT THIRTY YEARS OLD, MOUSTACHE.
 WHEN LAST SEEN WAS WEARING A HAT, BOW TIE,
 AND WAS CARRYING SOME PAPERS.
Can you spot him in one minute?

The UFO landed for a moment in the garden of the Embassy. Before it took off, some of its passengers hid in the trees.

The Ambassador isn't fooled. He knows Martians hide in the trees, but no one will believe him. Except you. The Ambassador thinks he spotted five Martians. How many of them can you find in the trees? (*2 minutes*)

STOP THE PRESSES

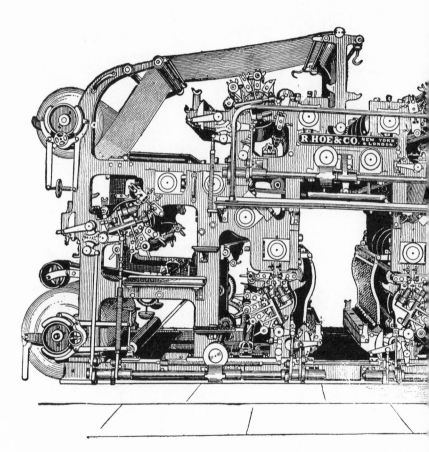

Mr. and Mrs. Em were working late one night at their printing press. Suddenly, an unpleasant beast from another planet arrived on the scene. Mr. and Mrs. Em hid. Can you find them? (*2 minutes*)

DOUBLE SPACE

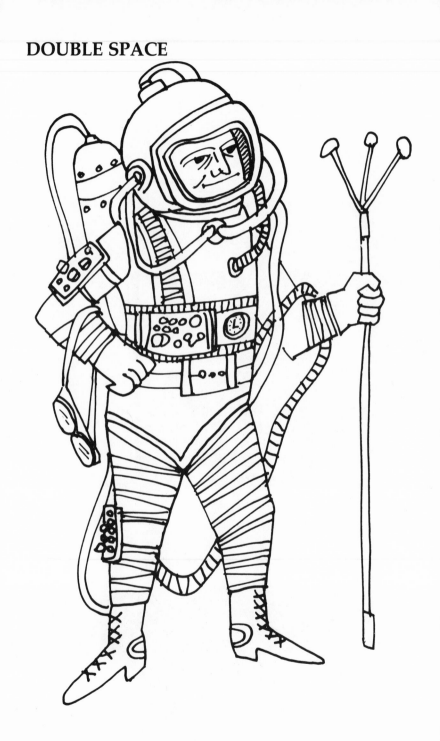

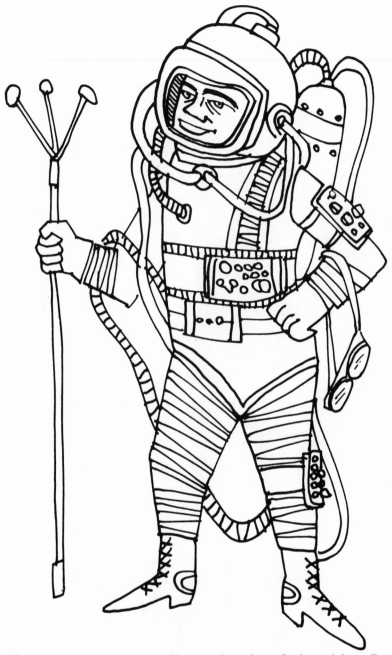

These two astronauts are all geared up for a flight to Mars. But each has forgotten a part of his equipment. Can you see what is missing from each? (*3 minutes*)

TEN TAILS

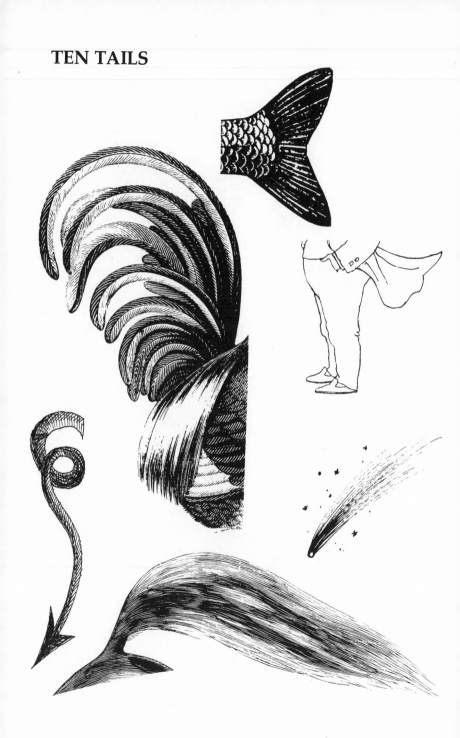

Every night for ten nights, Mrs. Queazy heard someone in her backyard. Each night she ran to the window just in time to see a different tail-end disappear over the fence. Here are pictures of what she saw, as drawn by the artist in the police department. Can you identify Mrs. Queazy's intruders?

UNIDENTIFIED FLYING OBJECT

Have you heard of this patient old gnome?
Through all outer space he would roam,
Past far-out space stations—
Through most constellations—
But where, oh, say, where, is his home?
  (*2 minutes*)

Time Flies

MISSING MATE

Mrs. MacMouse has lost her spouse,
Walking too far behind him.
When she got to the fair,
He wasn't there.
Can you help her find him? (*30 seconds*)

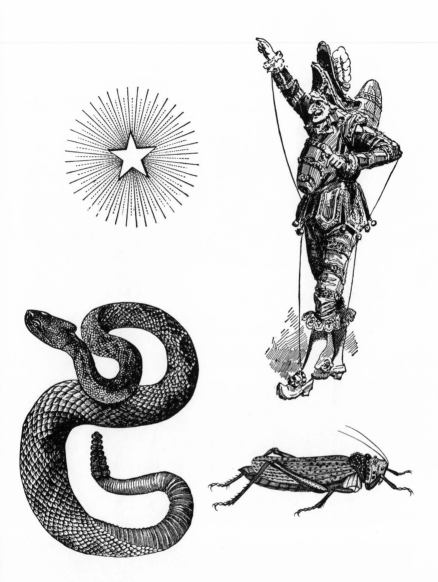

Of these ten objects, eight have something in common. What?
Which two do not fit in? (*2 minutes*)

SPARE PARTS

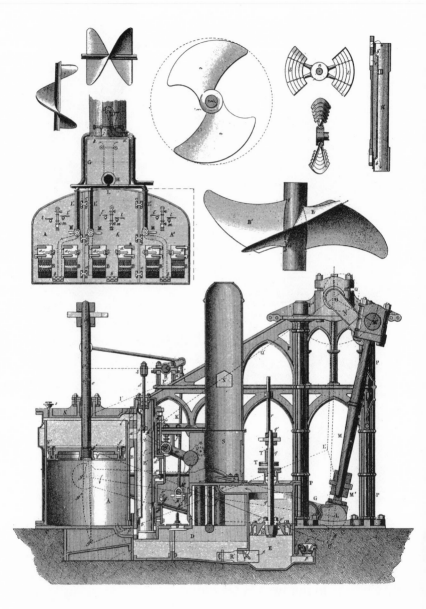

Rich Mr. Critch bought these expensive parts to build something in his spare time. Then he forgot what he was going to build. Can you tell him? (*1 minute*)

BIRDS IN HAND

How many birds can you count in thirty seconds?

CARELESS BO

Little Bo Peep has lost her sheep—and a lot of other barnyard friends, too. How many can you find? (*3 minutes*)

TOTE 'EM UP

Since Herman the Hermit has plenty of spare time (twenty-four hours a day), he whittled out this totem pole to give his message to the world. What is Herman trying to tell us? (*3 minutes*)

Each item on these pages has the word *cat* in its name. Can you identify them in four minutes?

There is something in this Christmas picture starting with each letter of the alphabet. How many can you list in five minutes? (You may use one item more than once—for example, a *drum* can also be a *toy*.)

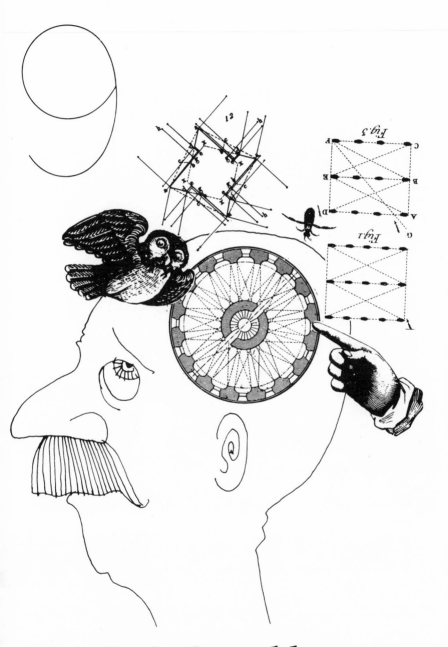

Brain Scramblers

MAKING TRACKS

Study these four people for a minute. Then turn the page.

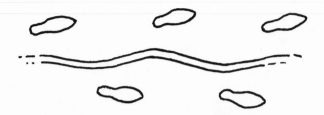

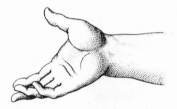

Which one made these tracks?

THE GREAT ART HEIST

Last week the museum had all of these valuable paintings on the south wall. This morning the museum was robbed and they were all taken. So was the book that told what was hanging on the wall. Take four minutes to study the next page. Then turn it.

1. How many pictures were on the wall?
2. How many were "abstract"?
3. How many had people in them?
4. How many had flowers or fruit?
5. How many had buildings?

CITYSCAPE

In five minutes, list as many items as you can which start with the letter S.

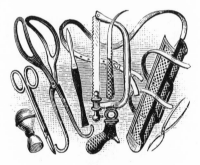

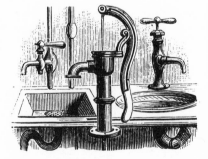

Theodore the Thief is thinking about going straight. But the prison library doesn't have any up-to-date books about careers. Theo is making his choice from an old book with old-time pictures. What is he thinking about doing?

THE PICTURE CLUES

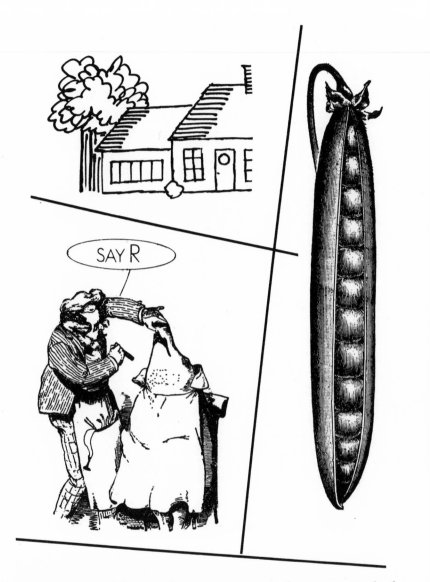

Sir Herbert Castleberry, the great anagram fan, was attacked in the library of his 97-room mansion. He desperately pulled these pages from his picture encyclopedia in order to tell who did it. Was it his butler, Peter Reinhart? Was it his sister, Constance Maplethorpe? Was it the chauffeur, Joseph H. Samuels? Was it the gardener, John Bliss? Or was it his neighbor, Michael Carrera? You have seven minutes on this one.

GONE FISHIN'

How many fishes can you count in two minutes?

Answers

PRIVATE EYES

The Line-Up—The third man from the left is "Mugsy."

They're Off . . .—The boy on stilts won.

The Tip—The note was made from words clipped from newspapers. It was written on Friday. The stolen item is "Mona Lisa," a painting. The word "thief" is misspelled. Three correct answers are good; four, great!

The Case of the Empty Ear—
The missing earring is at the lower left-hand corner of the jewelry box.

He Should Have Worn Gloves—The matching print is second from the right in the third row from the top.

SLYJINKS

Anyone Home?—Turn the picture upside down. On the left-hand page, you will see Dracula in the center of the picture at the bottom. His Gal Friday is on the right, her face in the wings of the large bat.

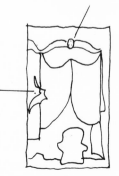

The Get-Away Car—Ohio. 27941. A horse. D.H.C. Two correct answers out of four is acceptable, but three means you're on the ball.

Put a Handle On It—A sword, brooms, a shovel, a watch, a faucet, a pump, pliers, a saw, a wheelbarrow, a spade, a sickle.

A score of five is fair, seven is okay, but eleven is 100%.

Going Buggy—

Two butterflies only are exactly alike. They look like this:

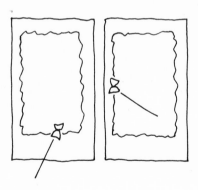

The acorn is not a bug or butterfly. The butterfly in the center of the top row (left-hand page) has only one wing.

You should have at least two correct answers.

Pen Pal—Dear Swanson: Be at the corner today at five o'clock. Bring the booty. Keep your cut and leave mine. (*signed*)
Three Fingers Fisher

THE EYES HAVE IT!

Masquerade—A clown, a gentleman, Mercury, a knight, a king, an explorer, a general. You should have gotten at least five correct. If you guessed all seven, you may wear the king's crown.

Mad Hatters—Mrs. Tew's hat is missing one butterfly and a beetle.

The Defective Detective—One tooth is cracked. The flame is missing from the torch of the Statue of Liberty. The chair has only three legs. The watch has two 9's. The microscope is missing the holder for the specimen. One rung is gone from the stepladder. The pitcher has a broken handle. The bicycle's seat is upside down.

If you found five flaws, you're good; seven would make you a Defective Detective First Class.

Time and Time Again—
1. Six
2. Seven
3. Two
4. Ten
5. Seven
6. The clock on the lower right-hand side of the left page is missing one hand.

This was a tough test, because there is so much detail in the timepieces, but you should have at least three correct answers.

Film Strip—2-3-5-4-1. The clues are the clock, the street numbers, the cat in the window, and the matching houses.

The Lost Heiress—Mrs. Potter's daughter can be seen by studying Mrs. Potter's nose. This sketch will help.

OOPS!

The Terrible Twins—The twins are the harmless looking gentlemen in glasses, in the upper left and low center.

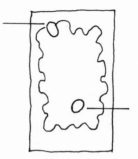

Lost Legs—A man, a sewing machine, a doll, a monkey, a spinning wheel, an elephant, a rooster, a horse, a beetle.

If you correctly identified six of the nine sets of legs, you are in the running. If you got them all, you're a winner.

Monster Mix and Match—

MINNIE MONSTER: a rooster's tail, a wig, a beetle's legs, a tooth, a peacock's tail, eyeglasses (with eyes).

JAZZY MONSTER: heads of two snakes, a lobster's legs, a French horn.

MALCOLM MONSTER: a stovepipe hat, eyeglasses (with eyes), a lobster, a pipe.

A good score? Five correct items on Minnie; two on Jazzy; all on Malcolm.

On the Loose—
Turn the book
upside down.
On the left-
hand page is a
lion, on the
right a snake
and a baby
elephant.

The Ghastly Garden—On the right-hand page is a hand and a
skull. (There is also a snake, which you may not consider
"horrible.") On the left-hand page is a man's head and a
floating foot.

Odd Bird—An eagle, a stork, an ostrich, a peacock. You
should get three out of four.

SNEAKS

Change of Heart—Hold the page flat at eye level and slowly
rotate it from left to right. The message reads: THE JEWELS
ARE IN THE ATTIC.

The Unlocked Window Caper—Stolen were the candlestick,
the deer's head, and a flower. Arrest the gentleman with the
cane, top hat, one black glove and the stolen flower in his
buttonhole. He left his other glove on the floor of the living
room.

Monster Rally—Turn the book upside down and you will see
the face of the *seventh* monster in the folds of the witch
lady's black sleeve.

Secret Plans—A bridge.

Double Exposure—There are eighteen members. You should
have been able to count at least fourteen in the two minutes.

The Would-Be Picasso—The artist has painted the five senses: Touch, sight, sound, smell, taste.

No Edison!—There are two valves and two wheels missing on Mr. Copicat's machine.

Name the Monster—

B for Barbells
A for Arrow (or Arm)
S for Skull
I for Ivory
L for Lantern
BASIL.

Master Mind—A general. These are plans for a military battle.

?-Star General—He is a three-star general.

The Can-Can Mystery—

*Can*taloupe
*Can*oe
*Can*teen
*Can*dy
*Can*delabra
*Can*vas
*Can*opy
*Can*non
*Can*nonballs
*Can*ary

If you figured out five of them, you should have tried a bit harder. Seven is excellent. Ten is the jackpot!

Mixed-Up Menagerie—

Top: lion, zebra.
Middle: rhinoceros, hyena.
Bottom: camel, giraffe, kangaroo.

If you get a score of five, you're all right; six is fine.(Almost no one guesses the hyena.).

CLOSE ENCOUNTERS

Find that Man!—The man you are after is third from the left in the second row.

Martians Branch Out—
There are seven Martians in the trees. (If you find five, the Ambassador will show you his medals. If you find seven, he'll give you one.)

Stop the Presses—Both Mr. and Mrs. Em are on the left-hand page. Their frightened faces are hidden in the machinery.

Double Space—The astronaut on the left is missing the hose which connects his helmet to the air tank on his back. The one on the right has no clock on his belt.

Ten Tails—Left-hand page: a fish, a rooster, a man, a devil, a comet, a horse.
Right-hand page: a dragon, an eel, a peacock, a pig.

Six correct answers are fair; eight are good; and all ten are as good as you can get!

Unidentified Flying Object—If you look closely, you'll see the letters that spell SATURN.

TIME FLIES

Missing Mate—Turn the picture upside down and there is Mr. MacMouse, looking very cross at being disturbed!

What's the Difference?—They all have legs—except the snake and the star.

Spare Parts—A steamboat.

Birds in Hand—Seventeen.

Careless Bo—
    One donkey
    One cow
    Three goats
    Two sheep
    Three roosters
Ten barnyard friends altogether. If you found five, that's pretty good; seven is very good, and nine, excellent.

Tote 'Em Up—Herman's message is in his totem figures from top to bottom:
    K is for Kitten
    E is for Elephant
    E is for Eagles
    P is for Plant
    O is for Owl
    U is for Unicorn
    T is for Tree
    KEEP OUT!

The Mystery of the Seven Cats—

    Cat-o-Nine-Tails
    *Cat*apult
    *Cat*tle
    *Cat*alogue
    *Cat*acomb
    *Cat*erpillar
    *Cat*aract

You might also say that the boy has made a *cat*ch of a *cat*fish! If you named three, you pass (barely); if you named six, you get an "A."

The A to Z Tree—Ark, Ball, Camel, Drum, Engine, Fish, Grapes, Horn, Ice Wagon, Jack-in-the-Box, Key, Locomotive, Monkey, Necklace, Ornament, Puppet, Queen, Racquet, Sword, Toy, Umbrella, Van, Wagon, Xylophone, Yacht, Zebra.

If you got ten, that's not bad, but you could do better. Fifteen is fine, twenty is tops.

(If you got all twenty-six, you may keep the tree and all the things on it.)

BRAIN SCRAMBLERS

Making Tracks—The man with the wheelbarrow.

The Great Art Heist—

1. Nine
2. Three
3. Four
4. Two
5. One

Two correct answers: fair; three, good; five, you're a winner.

Cityscape—

Sailboat	Sidewalk
Sailor	Sign
Sea	Sky
Seagulls	Skylight
Settee	Skyscrapers
Seller (of balloons)	Stairs
Shoes	Subway
Shoe Store	Sun

If you got ten out of these sixteen, you have "sharp eyes." If you got more than ten, you have *very* sharp eyes.

Study the picture again and this time list as many items as you can which begin with the letter B. There are at least eleven, but don't read this list until you have made up your own:

		Boat
	Bus	Birds
	Building	Banner
	Boy	Bank
	Book Store	Balloons
	Books	Ball

Tools of the Trade—Theodore is thinking about becoming a

Barber
Auctioneer
Carpenter
Surgeon
Upholsterer
Plumber
Cooper
Teacher
Mason
Butcher

Did you correctly identify five of these ten occupations? If so, so-so. If you guessed seven, that's good. If you got all ten (including *cooper*!), then your occupation should be Scholar.

The Picture Clues—

    tea - T
    yew - U
    eye - I
    bee - B
    jay - J
    sea - C
    ell - L
    ah - R
    peas - P

Put these letters in the correct order, and you'll see that the gardener, John Bliss, did the dirty deed. Herbert Castleberry's message was CULPRIT—J.B.

That was a rough one. If you got it, choose any score you like.

Gone Fishin'—You should net fourteen fish (the starfish counts). If you counted the octopus, throw him back (he's a mollusk).

If you caught at least ten fishes in two minutes, you did very well.

Index